THE
PONY

Don't miss any other
Young Corgi pony titles.

Also available now:

THE SCRUFFY PONY
by K.M. Peyton

THE PHANTOM PONY
by Peter Clover

Young Corgi books are designed especially with young readers in mind and are perfect for building reading confidence and stamina.

The Paradise Pony

K.M. Peyton

Illustrated by Robin Lawrie

YOUNG CORGI BOOKS

THE PARADISE PONY
A YOUNG CORGI BOOK : 0 552 55205 4

First publication in Great Britain

PRINTING HISTORY
Young Corgi edition published 1999

Set in Bembo MT Schoolbook

Young Corgi Books are published by Transworld Publishers,
61–63 Uxbridge Road, London W5 5SA,
a division of The Random House Group Ltd,
in Australia by Random House Australia (Pty) Ltd,
20 Alfred Street, Milsons Point, Sydney, NSW 2061, Australia,
and in New Zealand by Random House New Zealand Ltd,
18 Poland Road, Glenfield, Auckland 10, New Zealand
and in South Africa by Random House (Pty) Ltd,
Endulini, 5a Jubilee Road, Parktown 2193, South Africa.

Made and printed in Great Britain by
Cox & Wyman Ltd, Reading, Berkshire.

To Felix and Laetitia

Chapter One

No Rosette

Shona-Ilona Smith flew clear over all the jumps on her pony Lunar. The spectators clapped and cheered (mostly her parents and relations).

Lauren Briggs and her friend Tashy Parks scowled unsportingly. They hated Shona. She kept Lunar at a very expensive Equestrian Centre and had lessons with a Top Man. She was much too good to take part in the potty local show and was scooping all the prizes.

They – of course – kept their ponies in a field at home, had no lessons at all and their ponies had been obtained from a rescue centre. Lunar had cost ten thousand pounds!

"Even *I* could win on Lunar," said Tashy crossly. Her pony was called Monkey, because he was naughty. Nice, but naughty. If he was in a good mood, she stood a chance of winning, because he *could* jump if he felt like it. But with Lunar there, no-one else stood a chance.

"You're next," said Lauren.

Lunar had spoilt everything, she thought. Just shown them all up. One was supposed to compete for the sport – "Winning isn't everything" they always said. But to her friend Tashy it jolly well was. What was the point of entering if you didn't intend to win?

Monkey trotted happily into the ring and gave a cheerful buck. He was a fourteen-hand bay pony of unknown breeding. Just a pony, Tashy said, when asked. No smart papers or well-known sire. But his bright bay coat shone with good grooming and his glossy black mane and tail were combed out meticulously. All by Tashy, not a groom.

Tashy could be second, with luck, Lauren thought as her friend rode briskly at the first jump.

She was a very determined rider. Monkey jumped it, and then the second and third. So far so good.

Lauren watched anxiously. "Come *on*!" she muttered. Monkey was their best chance of beating beastly Shona. Of the two ponies Monkey was the most active. But Lauren could see that he was

already looking for a chance to duck out. Tashy knew this and pressed him on with her legs, her hands ready, driving for a rickety wall. Lunar had cleared it with a metre to spare. Monkey slowed down, Tashy shouted at him and he decided to jump after all. He crashed through it, scattering wooden bricks far and wide, and cantered on, bucking happily.

Lauren groaned. But now Tashy was angry and Monkey knew it, and decided to be good. He jumped the rest clear, and Tashy rode back to them, trying to look like a good loser. Not very successfully.

Lauren shouted, "Bad luck, Tashy," in a sporting way. But they both knew it had nothing to do with luck. It was just Monkey.

Lauren went in on her pony Humpfrey and he refused three times at the first, and she rode out again, red-faced.

She was really miserable. Humpfrey never seemed very eager to jump. Lauren tried to make excuses for him. He was old, after all, about eighteen, and was far from being a thoroughbred like Lunar. He was a sort of Welsh pony, white (or usually off-white), thirteen-two hands high, and very kind. Lauren loved him dearly. But at shows he always made her really unhappy.

"I don't know why I bother to enter!"

Tashy made her, that's why. After all, it was fun to ride to the show together – it was only in the local village – and stand around nattering with their friends.

There were several more clear rounds so Lauren knew that Tashy wasn't going to get a rosette. They took their ponies and tied them to the hedge and settled down to eat their sandwiches while the jump-off took place. Most of the ponies had come in horseboxes, and Lunar would be taken home in the vast lorry belonging to the Whitemarket Equestrian Centre. This place was only a mile down the road, opposite the farm where Lauren lived. Tashy lived in the village, but kept Monkey at Lauren's with Humpfrey.

It was a warm summer day and the sandwiches were good (tuna and tomato) and Lauren and Tashy soon cheered up.

"After all, I wouldn't want to ride like Shona does," Lauren said. "Round and round that manège every day, getting shouted at by Horrid Hector."

Horrid Hector was really Mr H. Harbottle, chief instructor at Whitemarket. Shona had a lesson every day after school. Her mother brought her in a white Mercedes. The car usually passed Tashy on her bicycle, going to the farm.

"We have more fun," Lauren agreed. No lessons, but they seemed to stay on all right, even when bareback, which they often were. The farm went down through woods to the sea, and there were sand-dunes to ride over, and a beach of hard sand to gallop on. The Equestrian Centre only had the indoor and outdoor schools and two measly acres of grass.

"Round and round in circles. That's all they do," Lauren said. "Poor things."

"Winning isn't everything," Tashy agreed.

But in their hearts, although they didn't say so, they longed for ponies that would win rosettes, and trot along with their noses in their chests, pointing their toes. Humpfrey trailed along with his head down and nose out, for all Lauren's efforts. And Monkey . . . Monkey went backwards, bucked or sometimes wouldn't go at all.

"What do you expect, for nothing?" Mr Briggs said rather crossly, if he heard them wishing. "You're lucky to have ponies at all."

Farming was bad, money was short. Free rescue ponies was all they could manage. Shona's father was a financial consultant, whatever that was. "It means you consult him, and he takes your money," said Mr Briggs. "He just sits at a desk, taking money."

"Why don't you do that then?" Lauren asked.

Mr Briggs laughed. "I'm not clever enough."

But Lauren and Tashy couldn't see the cleverness in keeping Lunar in such an expensive stable and getting Shona shouted at every day. Sometimes Shona burst into tears. Lauren and Tashy

watched through a hole in the fence to see if they could pick up any tips from Horrid Hector's instructions. Shona saw them once and came over and bent down and shouted at them. The next day the hole was boarded up. So that finished their only chance of learning something.

But Shona did win a lot of rosettes. Lunar was black, just under fourteen hands, and won a lot of show classes as well as jumping. Shona just came to ride him. He was already saddled and bridled when she came, and she never had to muck out or groom. She didn't know anything about feeding, or what to do with a nail in the foot, or a bit of colic.

"I bet she wishes she kept her pony with us and just messed about with Lunar," Tashy said. "Messed about like we do."

"At least we never feel like crying."

"Only at horse shows," said Tashy, and laughed.

So they rode home, rosetteless. They had to pull into the hedge to make way for the Whitemarket horsebox. It was driven by Horrid Hector (Shona had gone home in the Mercedes). The horsebox windscreen was framed with colourful rosettes, and Hector gave them a cold nod.

"Yuk," said Tashy.

Tashy was really called Natasha and her parents hated animals and lived in the village in a flat full of computers. Natasha was a great disappointment to them. Their only child, she was stocky and scowling, with straight black hair that seemed to stick out in tufts, and sharp black eyes. Her parents were both professors, and Tashy was clever but would not work at school. She spent all her time drawing, or down on the farm with Monkey. They threatened quite often to take Monkey away, send him back to the rescue home.

"But they never will," Mr Briggs said. "He keeps Tashy out of their hair."

"Don't they love her?" Lauren asked.

"Yes, I'm sure they do, but she isn't the nice little girl they would like."

"Like I am?"

"Yes, darling," said her mother, and laughed.

Certainly Lauren did not seem to get into trouble like Tashy. Lauren was quiet and good-natured and patient.

"It's not that we don't love our ponies," said Tashy. "We just wish they were *better*."

"And I bet Shona wishes Lunar was nicer."

"Yes, I bet she does. He's beastly. He bites. At least neither of ours is nasty."

"No. They're lovely," said Lauren staunchly.

But, inside, they both wished their ponies WOULD WIN ROSETTES!

Chapter Two
"There's something funny in the yard"

They rode past the smart drive of the Whitemarket Equestrian Centre and into the back drive of Smallgains Farm (very well-named, according to Mr Briggs). They kept their ponies in an old stockyard near the road. It was now disused, the roofs being too low for modern machinery, and the stock now housed in new barns up by the farmhouse. The farmhouse was further along the drive, quite a way away. The girls had the stockyard completely for their own use.

"It's a palace," Mr Briggs said when the ponies came from the rescue place. And the rescue people agreed. A whole yard to themselves, with mangers full of hay, and straw laid down from the big round bales.

Better by far than stuffy Whitemarket, where all the looseboxes were inside,

with rails all round, and nowhere for the horses to look out.

"Like being in prison," said Lauren.

The stockyard had open sheds on three sides. The fourth side was fenced, with a gate into the paddock. One of the open sheds had been divided by Mr Briggs into three separate stables, but mostly the ponies lived loose. Water and electricity were laid on. The girls had

made a tack room out of one of the boxes, and had an old sofa in there and a kettle and tea and a tin of biscuits filched from home. Also a transistor radio, a pile of magazines, tapes, and on the walls pin-ups which varied weekly. All it needed, said Mrs Briggs, was a phone line to the farmhouse so that she could tell them when tea was ready.

"And we could say, bring it down," said Lauren.

"Very funny," said Mrs Briggs.

But no-one could deny that it was, indeed, a palace, a haven of their own.

The show had been so disappointing, they almost opted to go for a ride down to the sea to forget about it. But there wasn't really time, if Tashy was to get home in time for supper. So they untacked the ponies and tied them up to give them a rub down before turning them out into the paddock.

It was a routine job, coming back home from a ride, but somehow, tonight, there was a funny atmosphere in the yard. The ponies wouldn't stand still and kept putting up their heads and staring nervously into the distance. Lauren felt a strange cold wind on the back of her neck and Humpfrey turned sharply to look behind her and trod on her foot.

She yelled out.

At the same moment Monkey put up his head and whinnied. He seemed to be whinnying to another pony, but not to Humpfrey. He was looking towards the gate.

"Whatever's got into them?" Lauren asked.

The sun was low over the woods and the fields were touched with a soft pink glow. You couldn't see the sea from the stockyard as the woods were in the way. But, if you could, Lauren knew it would be fiery-gold and magnificent, just needing angels in the sky and choirs singing to set off how it made her feel. Sometimes she just sat on Humpfrey and looked at things like that, but Tashy would never wait. She never noticed.

But this time, even *she* noticed. "There's something funny in the yard," she said.

"Ghosts. The ponies are seeing ghosts," Lauren said, as Humpfrey pulled at his headcollar, looking frightened.

When they turned them loose, the two ponies stood huddled together, sniffing the wind, ears pricked. Usually they started grazing as if they hadn't eaten for a week.

"There's something around that's frightening them."

They stared down the field, but there was nothing to be seen. Sometimes a fox would set them off, or a deer. But this evening the field was still and empty.

"It feels funny," Lauren said.

Tashy shrugged. It was too stupid! "I've got to go home, else I'll be in trouble," she said. "We're imagining things."

"I'll come down before I go to bed," Lauren said. "To see it's all right."

They used bicycles to go backwards and forwards from the farm and up and down from the village. Lauren rode home and went in for supper and her brother Paul jeered, "Where are the rosettes then?" He knew they wouldn't have any. They never did.

"We left them in the tack room," Lauren said. "Hundreds of them."

"Never mind, dear," said their mother. "I'm sure you enjoyed yourselves."

"Yes, we did," said Lauren staunchly. "I'd rather have Humpfrey than that Lunar any day." (If only he would *jump* like Lunar!)

Lauren went back to the stockyard as dusk was falling, to see if the ponies had settled. A farmer's daughter, she was not afraid of being outside in the dark. She loved the smell of the dewy fields and the silent white shape of the barn owl hunting over the hedges. You saw more at dusk and dawn than in the bright light of day.

But when she got to the yard this time, she was frightened. There was a presence – you could *feel* it – something moving, something breathing. The cold breath. Then silence. A rustling in the straw. A soft whicker – was it her imagination? The ponies were down the field out of sight, yet Lauren felt there was a pony in the yard.

"What are you?" she cried out.

She stood bravely. "Are you a ghost?"

And the answer came quite clearly:

"Yes, I'm a ghost, and I'm hungry. I want a feed."

"Where are you?" Lauren cried, all the hairs on the back of her neck standing up with a fright. Did ghosts eat?

"Here. I'm over here."

And Lauren looked to where the voice came from, in the darkest corner of the barn, and as she looked a pony took shape. From total darkness a soft grey form came into being – of a pony more beautiful by far even than Lunar. It was a grey mare, a smoky dappled grey, of perfect proportions, with a fine head, lustrous eyes, a long silky mane sweeping her shoulder and beautiful thoroughbred legs. The pony stood looking at her, trembling.

Lauren gaped. She felt her jaw drop open.

The pony said, "I'm Cobweb. I lived here once."

Lauren had no words. The pony was so beautiful! She now looked quite real, gazing at her with her great eyes.

"I had to come back. I've nowhere else to go. I've been banished. He said go away and haunt someone, in a really nasty voice. So here I am. But I don't want anyone to be frightened. I've never haunted before."

"Who banished you?"

"Tocker. He's the boss, the Paradise boss."

"Tocker?" Lauren thought she must be dreaming. *Another* ghost? "And Paradise . . . where's Paradise?"

"Paradise," said Cobweb, "is where all ponies go when their lives down here are over. I thought everyone knew that."

"And Tocker?"

"I tell him the truth. He doesn't like it."

"What truth?"

"Oh, that he's a bully and braggart and a pain in the bottom. It's all true, and everyone knows it's true, but none of the others dare say it. They all tell him he's wonderful. But they don't shine."

"Shine?"

"If you tell the truth you shine all over, like a beacon. You look magic. When I told Tocker he was a bully, they could all see me shining, so bright they could hardly look at me. So they all knew it was true, what I was saying. And they were all frightened and said, 'No, no, Tocker, it's not true! You are wonderful!' But not a single one of them shone. They just went dull, even duller the more they said he was wonderful. And so, of course, Tocker was really cross and banished me."

"But Tocker – what is Tocker?"

"Tocker is a Welsh cob. You know how terribly bossy they are? He can't help it really, being so beautiful and strong and wild. Everyone does what he says. He's got a good heart, will help any animal in trouble, but if you cross him he has this wild streak – gets terribly uppity. He's been spoilt, looking so handsome. He's got used to being doted on and always getting his own way. So, when I tell him the truth – I was the only one brave enough – he sends me away! To teach me a lesson, he said!"

To Lauren's amazement, big tears like pearl drops ran from Cobweb's eyes.

"I came here. Because I was happy here, once."

"When? When were you here?"

"Oh, a long time ago. I belonged to a boy called Billy Briggs."

"Billy Briggs is my great-grandfather! I remember him, when I was little! But he's dead now."

"Oh, he would be, like me. It was a long time ago."

"Oh, don't be unhappy! I'll look after you! Honestly, our ponies are really happy, this is a good place."

Lauren felt desperate, seeing this heavenly pony looking so sad. She might be a ghost, but she said she was hungry. Lauren fetched a feed in Humpfrey's bucket and put it down before her. Cobweb's tears ceased flowing and she stuck her lovely muzzle into the feed just like a real (greedy) pony. She looked more solid now, like a proper pony, as if her ghostliness was wearing off.

Or was she – Lauren – dreaming? If she came back in the morning with Tashy, would Tashy see her too? Lauren thought her mind was going, and in the morning she would find it all a hallucination.

"Are you staying?" she asked.

"Well, would you mind?"

"Mind! Of course not! Having *you* . . ." An honour, a blessing, a heavenly gift! Grovel, grovel. What a pony! Hers? Lauren's brain reeled.

She put a haynet up for her.

"Tocker told me to stay away until I could apologize. But I won't! He expected me to climb down, you see, so as not to be banished. But I wouldn't. I think he was very surprised when I went. He might come looking for me, if we're unlucky. He likes to go haunting. But I don't very much. I don't like scaring people. He thinks it's a great joke."

Tocker sounded rather like Monkey.

"Your ponies are rather nervous of me. But I'll keep away from them until they get used to me."

"Oh, yes, they aren't nasty. Only the bay, Monkey – he can be a bit naughty sometimes."

She told Cobweb about their disastrous day at the village show. It was nice talking to a pony that talked back. She told her about the all-conquering Lunar.

"Oh, I know that sort," said Cobweb. "So conceited! We've got lots up there. They can't help it, I suppose, those show-jumpers. Billy and me – we won a lot in our day. But I don't go round *telling* everyone."

Now she had eaten, and saw that Lauren was a friend, Cobweb had stopped being nervous. She looked quite solid now, not like a ghost any more. Lauren asked her about it, and Cobweb said she could disappear again without any trouble. Still be there, but invisible. "Like I was when you came home. I was in the field, near the gate. I let your ponies see me," she said. "I can come and go, no trouble. It's up to me who sees me and who doesn't. It's just magic. Ghosts are like that."

"Will you be here in the morning, when Tashy comes? Tashy's my friend. She owns Monkey."

"If you don't send me away, yes."

"However could I send you away? You are so – so beautiful!"

"Yes, I'm very well-bred. But it's a kind heart that matters. Animals or humans, it's the same. If Tocker comes – oh, you wait till you see Tocker!"

"Will Tocker come?"

"If I don't go back . . . he's so nosy. He'll want to know what I'm up to. He really didn't expect me to go. I think he'll be sorry now."

Lauren knew she had to go home: it was past her bedtime. "Please be here in the morning! We'll look after you!"

"Thank you," said Cobweb. "Yes, I'll stay."

Lauren cycled slowly back to the farmhouse.

She thought she was dreaming. Her head reeled. It was magic, a magic pony! But how could it be for real, a pony that talked?

"I'm going bonkers," she told herself. And went indoors.

Chapter Three
Try to Ride a Ghost

Lauren didn't say anything about her vision when she got home.

But as she was going to bed she said to her father, "Did your grandfather have a pony?"

"Of course he had a pony. How else would he get about? Went to school on a pony."

"What was it like?"

"However should I know? I never asked him."

Mrs Briggs said, "Auntie Mabel would know – Great-Auntie Mabel. She'll talk about the old days till the cows come home. Since old Billy died, she's got all the old photos and things."

"All she will talk about, the past," Mr Briggs complained. "Drives you up the wall."

"It's interesting, if you've got the time," Mrs Briggs said mildly. Mr Briggs was nearly always in a bad temper, farming being what it was. "Go and have a chat with your great-auntie Mabel, dear. Or should I say, your great-great-auntie Mabel. She's nearly ninety, after all. She'll tell you all about the horses here, in those days. She can't remember what day of the week it is, but she remembers all that old stuff."

"The farm was rich in her day," Mr Briggs growled. "They all lived like kings. Pity we weren't born then."

"We're fine, dear. Stop growling."

Lauren was used to the way her parents carried on. Auntie Mabel lived in a cottage in the village, and was still pretty spry, even if she didn't remember what day of the week it was. Lauren decided she would go and visit as soon as she could. Tomorrow! Tomorrow was Sunday.

She woke up early and raced down to the stockyard (at least, raced as far as the bumpy lane permitted). It was a clear, dewy morning with a faint mist over the fields. The ponies had left long trails in the grass. As usual they were down the field, not bothered about coming unless she called them with a bucket of feed. She leapt off her bike and stared.

Two ponies grazing, and one other, on its own. Two very ordinary, unhandsome ponies – and one apart, rosy grey in the dawn light. A dream pony, ghost pony, heavenly Cobweb – she was still there!

It wasn't a dream!

Lauren called out. Cobweb put up her head and pricked her ears. Immediately she started to come up the field. The other ponies stared after her and slowly, one by one, followed.

Lauren let them into the yard. Cobweb stood in the field, waiting.

"Do you want to come in?" Lauren asked.

"No, I'll stay here until they're used to me. I don't want to be kicked by that Monkey. I'd like a feed though."

"We don't feed them much in the summer. Only a few nuts. But you can have a proper feed, if you like."

"I'm used to Paradise grass, you see. Your grass is nothing like Paradise grass."

"Well, no."

Lauren thought their grass was very good, but no doubt Paradise grass was something special. She fetched Cobweb a bucket of feed and the other ponies stood in the yard watching her crossly, wanting feed too.

"You're too fat," Lauren told them, which was true. No wonder they couldn't lift their fat tummies over the jumps. Lunar was sleek and spare like a racehorse. The poor pony never went out in a field.

"You won't go away?" Lauren said to Cobweb. She couldn't wait to see what Tashy would say when she saw this heavenly visitor.

"No. I'm staying here. I like it here."

"I've got to go home for breakfast. Then I'll be back, and Tashy will come."

"Fine by me," said Cobweb.

Tashy was as bowled over as Lauren had been the night before. She had never seen a pony so beautiful, not even Lunar. A *ghost* pony! It took her ages to get over the shock, just like Lauren.

"Oh, what must she be like to ride?" Tashy breathed. Monkey was so lumpy and uncomfortable! "Can we try?"

"Ask her," said Lauren.

Tashy asked and Cobweb said doubtfully, "Well, you can try, but I can't promise anything."

Tashy ran to fetch a saddle. Humpfrey's should fit her, although it might be a bit wide. Lauren slid it over Cobweb's back.

But it fell straight through her onto the ground.

They tried again and the same thing happened.

Cobweb looked round and said, "I'm sorry. I can't help it. I am a ghost, after all."

Tashy slid on her bareback, from the gate, and landed in a heap under Cobweb's feet.

"Terribly sorry," said Cobweb.

"What a pity we can't ride you!"

"But come with us! You must come!"

So they saddled up Monkey and Humpfrey and set off down their usual track towards the sea. Cobweb came along behind, trotting like a show pony, gliding over the rough ground with her nose tucked in and her lovely long mane blowing in the breeze. Then she went on ahead, and the other ponies started to behave much better. Monkey stopped dancing about and bucking and started to trot steadily, and Humpfrey pulled himself together and became all collected under Lauren's legs – so much more comfortable!

"What a good influence she is!" Tashy shouted.

Lauren thought Cobweb might be able to induce Humpfrey to *jump*! Their ponies certainly knew Cobweb was there. But whether they could see her or not Lauren couldn't tell.

Tashy said, "If they go so much better with her in front, if she came to a show with us they might win!"

"She'd have to make herself invisible – otherwise everyone would just shout, 'Loose horse!'"

It was a wonderful idea. Because when they came to quite difficult places where the ponies sometimes had trouble, with Cobweb in front they flew over without hesitation. And when they got home and practised over their 'show-jumps' (branches on rickety old oil cans), Humpfrey and Monkey jumped just like

Lunar, with miles to spare. Cobweb flew over in front of them, showing the way. It was as if some of Cobweb's magic had got into the ponies.

When they unsaddled Lauren asked Cobweb about coming to a show with them.

"When is it?"

"There's one within riding distance in a fortnight."

"Oh, I shall probably be gone by then!"

"Oh, don't go!" they pleaded. "Please stay here!"

"In a fortnight . . . ?" Cobweb was doubtful. "Tocker will come looking by then, I should think. He's very hasty when he's cross, but afterwards, quite quickly, he's sorry. He's probably expecting me back quite soon."

"And if you don't go?"

"He'll come and fetch me. He's so bossy. We all do what he wants in the end. He says it was the same when he was alive too."

Tashy and Lauren exchanged glances. *Two* heavenly ponies! What bliss!

"*Do* stay!" they pleaded.

"Well certainly, if I can. It's a nice change here. It can get a bit boring in Paradise, so lovely all the time."

With that they had to be content. The ponies were rubbed down and turned out, and wandered away down the field. Two ponies together, and one apart, a ghost pony. A beautiful ghost.

Chapter Four

Auntie Mabel's Story

"Let's go and talk to Auntie Mabel," Lauren said as soon as they were finished. "Dad says she knows all about the horses that were here once. He said she will remember Cobweb."

"And that Tocker she talks about . . ."

They rode to the village on their bikes. They passed the Whitemarket Equestrian Centre and looked over the fence and saw Shona-Ilona Smith going round in circles in the manège.

"I thought she'd get a day off on Sundays!"

They felt quite sorry for her, in spite of all her rosettes. She never looked happy on Lunar, just all screwed-up.

"We could run a livery stable," Tashy said. "And she could have fun with us. And pay us."

Lauren thought this rather a good idea.

Auntie Mabel was really surprised to see them. And very pleased. She was an active old lady, farm-bred, and used to milking cows in the days of her youth. She rattled round the kitchen fetching out biscuits and making cocoa. They made polite conversation for a bit, and then Lauren asked if they could see her old photos of the farm.

Her eyes lit up. "Why, of course, my dears!"

Nobody wanted to know, usually. She brought out a large cardboard box and emptied it out on the table. Piles of faded sepia pictures, of show-winning cows, ladies in long dresses and large hats, lots of men posing with guns . . .

"Is there one of your brother Billy? He used to ride a pony."

"Billy. Aye. Let's see . . ." *Shuffle, shuffle* . . .

"Did he have a pony called Cobweb?"

"Yes he did. A grey mare. A topping little pony."

And there she was, staring at the camera with her great lustrous eyes which even the faded photograph could not hide. Astride her, with long stirrups and feet well forward, sat a boy of about twelve, very cocksure. His eyes too were shining and confident. What a pair! Lauren thought. Even in the frail old photo their life and confidence shone through.

"He was never off her back. Went

everywhere on her, and the prizes they won! Father was very proud of him. Jumping and showing – at the old Aggie in London. They used to go up on the train, the two of them."

"The Aggie?"

"The old Agricultural Hall, that was. In Islington. That's where they had the big horse shows then. Great names were there, and he beat 'em! Beat 'em all."

"Fancy going up to London for a show!" Tashy said. "From here!" And on a train!

"They had horseboxes on the ends of trains in those days. Always two or three, for the horses."

There was Cobweb again, posing against a high brick wall with two rosettes on her browband. Just like Lunar.

"If only we could ride her!" whispered Tashy.

But Lauren had another enquiry. "Was there ever a pony called Tocker at Smallgains?"

"Tocker? Yes, but he was before the photographs. My grandfather – that was in the early eighteen-forties – oh, a long time ago! But I remember a story he told about a pony called Tocker. A right funny story it was."

"What happened?"

"Grandfather was a great horseman. He had driving ponies; he used to drive, not ride, because he had a gammy knee. He couldn't ride. This story he told – he had this new driving pony, Tocker. Very high-spirited he was, young and strong. Had a will of his own. One day Grandfather harnessed him up and set off with Billy to visit another farm. They had to go along the farm tracks, over the fields. Well, Tocker decided he didn't want to go that way and he stopped in the middle of a field and wouldn't go on. Nothing would make him go on, not coaxing or whipping or shouting. So Grandfather sent Billy off to the nearest farm for a fencing stake and a mallet, and he knocked the post into the ground and tied Tocker to it.

Then he walked home and Billy went with him. And he didn't go back until the next afternoon. There was Tocker, still tied short to the fencing post, not able to graze or anything. And Grandfather untied him and got in the trap, and off went Tocker as good as gold. And he never stopped like that again. Not ever."

The girls digested this story. It was a good one. Did Cobweb know about it? Lauren wondered. It was the sort of story that the boastful Tocker would not like to hear, she guessed.

"How come you know about these ponies then?" Auntie Mabel asked. "Your dad been telling you these old tales?"

"Mmm," Lauren mumbled. How

could she tell Auntie Mabel about their ghost? Auntie Mabel had all her marbles, and would never believe them.

"It's all them motor-bikes and fast cars now. But the young men, then, like Billy, they loved their horses like the young men love their motor-bikes. Showed off on 'em. When Billy grew out of Cobweb he was heartbroken. He never had another as good, not ever."

"What happened to her?"

"Oh, they sold her for a lot of money. I don't know who to."

Auntie Mabel started piling the photos back into their box. "Pity your father never bought you good ponies," she said, rather witheringly. "Only those old scrap-heaps."

Lauren and Tashy might criticize their ponies to each other, but when someone else criticized them – "They're not scrap-heaps!" they cried in unison.

Auntie Mabel laughed. "Well, they

make you happy, that's what matters."

Yes, that's what mattered.

But they couldn't help thinking enviously of their great-grandfather Billy on the heavenly Cobweb, and all those rosettes.

"We'll have to make a plan," Tashy said. "To get Cobweb to help us. They went so well with her this morning! I want to beat Lunar at the next show. See their faces! Horrid Hector and Mummy Smith!"

"Yes!" cried Lauren. "I'm sure Cobweb will think of something! . . . Before she goes back," she added.

"Before Tocker comes to fetch her," Tashy said.

Chapter Five

Tocker Arrives!

Lauren was a kind girl, and did not tell Cobweb the story about Tocker. Poor Tocker! He would hate it.

But Cobweb was getting worried about staying until the show. The novelty of coming back as a ghost was beginning to wear off. She was hankering for Paradise grass again, and Paradise weather, and the delicious water of clear running streams and all her Paradise friends.

"But you were happy on earth once," Lauren said.

"I was happy with Billy."

"What happened afterwards, when you were sold?"

"It was never the same afterwards," Cobweb said. "I don't want to talk about it." And she faded as she spoke and looked as if she was just a shadow against the darkening hedgerow.

Lauren felt herself give a little shiver: the pony's feelings were infectious. She thought how awful, if someone sold her off to somewhere else! Let's not think about it . . .

"Please stay!"

So Cobweb stayed, and every day they practised their jumps. With Cobweb going in front, their ponies flew over everything. Even Humpfrey, grunting with the effort, lifted his stiff legs high and went over as if on wings. Perhaps he had sprouted invisible ones! Lauren could believe anything now.

But one morning when she went down early to the stockyard, she saw something that made her catch her breath. It was going to be hot, but the hedges were sparkling with dew and her boots made long trails in the wet grass. The ponies were at the very bottom of the field, half hidden in a dawn mist that lay in gauzy streamers across the dip. They seemed to have no legs, only their backs showing, drifting as if on a sea. They weren't grazing, their heads were up, gazing away towards the woods. Cobweb, still slightly apart, whinnied softly.

And out of the mist, from the direction of the sea, a pony appeared. And the mist rolled away in front of him as if the brightness of his coat was melting it, as if it was afraid to hide such a beautiful pony.

He was the bright chestnut of polished copper, built like a little war-horse, with a flowing silver mane and tail. He lifted his legs high and arrogantly, and arched his neck and his whole demeanour said, "Look at me! Stand aside! Here I am!"

And Monkey and Humpfrey wheeled round – if this was a ghost they could certainly see him quite plainly – and galloped away. But Cobweb reared up and whinnied, and went towards him, floating through the mist with her lovely stride.

"Tocker!" Lauren breathed.

He had come to take Cobweb away! And you could see she was so pleased to see him, cavorting around him with little snorts of delight, while he stood bossily, head up, tossing his mane, laying down the law.

Lauren half expected them to dissolve there and then, or gallop away through the mist, and she shouted down the field, "Cobweb! Don't go! Don't go!"

And the despair in her voice made the two ponies look towards her. Lauren saw the hesitation, their anxiety to be gone, and she was sure that in a moment they would fade from her view for ever, and she cried out again: "Please! Cobweb! *Tocker!*"

And Tocker pranced round at the sound of his name, and looked straight at her and she knew then that he was curious.

She ran down the field towards them.

"I haven't got all day," Tocker said when she was within earshot. "What do you want?"

"Don't take Cobweb away!"

"She's been away far too long. It's not allowed." He tossed his head and stamped a front hoof. "I don't allow it!"

What a brilliant pony he was! Even Lunar would fade to nothing beside this glowing animal with his great flashing eyes.

Lauren tried tact. "Just till after breakfast? I've come to feed you. We've got some very good feed, haven't we, Cobweb?"

"Well, yes, the food's very good here," Cobweb said. "Not the grass, compared with home. But the stuff in buckets – that's very tasty. Better than we had in our day here."

"Plain oats we had then," Tocker said.

"They feed something called 'mix' today," Cobweb said. "And nuts. Try them. We can go later."

Tocker stopped looking quite so bossy, and dropped his nose meekly and said,

"OK, I'll stay for breakfast."

Lauren went back up the field and got four buckets of feed. (Their dad would ask where it had all gone later, when they ran out. But she couldn't help that now.)

"It's still good here, like it used to be," Cobweb told Tocker. "That's why I've stayed so long. Nice people. Nice ponies. I've been teaching them to jump."

"Huh!" snorted Tucker, his nose in the bucket.

But Lauren got the idea that he was no longer so keen to go. He was curious, looking all round him.

"Where have all the cattle gone?"

"We keep them up by the milking parlour, nearer the house."

"Milking *parlour*? Whatever's that?"

Lauren didn't think she could start to explain how milking by machinery worked. It was all done by hand in his day.

She changed the subject. "Cobweb's been teaching our ponies to jump. We need her to stay just a bit longer really, to get them to win at the show."

"You get many rosettes?" Tocker looked witheringly at Monkey and Humpfrey eating their feeds. "I shouldn't think so, with those." He said 'those' with great disdain.

Lauren was rather cross. "They do their best. They can't help it if they're not as beautiful as you."

Tocker looked pleased. Lauren could see that he was very conceited.

"I was never beaten in my day. I always won the championships."

"Did you jump?"

"Jump? I could jump a house. Five-barred gates out hunting, nothing stopped me. Never."

"It's only three days to the show. If you stayed and helped we could beat Shona-Ilona Smith."

"Who's Shona-Ilona Smith?" He was very inquisitive.

Lauren explained about the wonderful Lunar and how Cobweb was going to go invisible and make their ponies do clear rounds.

"Three days? I can't hang around here that long," Tocker said.

Lauren sat on the fence watching the four ponies. Tocker and Cobweb, the magic visitors, stayed slightly apart. Lauren knew it was all a dream; next week they would be back to normal. But if they had two red rosettes to hang in the tack room, it would be real. If they could beat Lunar . . .

But Tocker wouldn't stay. "Very good grub, but we've got to go. Nice to meet you," he said.

And Lauren remembered the story Great-Auntie Mabel had told them about Tocker. She had a wonderful idea. She jumped off the fence. "Before you go, I want to say something to Cobweb."

She walked away and Cobweb went with her, while Tocker chased Monkey off his bucket and finished Monkey's feed.

Lauren told Cobweb Auntie Mabel's story about Tocker being tied to the post.

Cobweb was goggle-eyed at the gossip and highly amused. "What a laugh! Poor old Tocker!"

"I wasn't going to tell you. But if you tell Tocker you know about it, you could make him stay. Say that if he doesn't stay and help us you'll tell the story to the others. And you will shine, and everyone will know it's true. I don't think he'd like it."

"I'll say he wouldn't! He'd go mad!"

"Would you make him stay then? Tell him you know the story?"

Cobweb looked doubtfully towards the chestnut pony, now hogging Humpfrey's feed. "Yes, why not?" she said. "I don't mind staying, after all. If we both go into the ring, and Tocker comes behind them, believe me, your ponies will jump *everything* with miles to spare." Cobweb giggled. "Yes. It's really funny. I'll tell him."

When Tocker had finished what was

left of Humpfrey's feed he tossed his head at Cobweb and said, "We'll be off then."

"Just a minute," said Cobweb.

Lauren collected up the empty buckets and pretended to take no notice of what was going on. But when she glanced over her shoulder at the two ponies she saw that Cobweb was *shining* – she was almost impossible to look at, so bright was her coat, like the best silver with the full moon sparkling on her elegant flanks. Anyone could see she was telling the truth! And Tocker – Tocker had lost all his bounce and Lauren could see the dismay in the droop of his head and the horror in his eyes.

She heard him say, "You can't come back and say all that to them!"

"I will if you don't stay until the show," Cobweb said stoutly.

Lauren saw that it took a lot of courage for her to say this. But she looked so strong and so beautiful, glittering in the morning sun, holding up her head in defiance, that Lauren's heart went out to her. Even if it didn't work, she couldn't have done more to help.

"Three days?" Tocker was saying crossly. "Well, I suppose if you *need* me so much . . ."

He turned his back, switching his tail irritably. "I meant to stay a bit, actually," he said. "See what the old place is like these days. I liked it here, once."

Almost at once he began to perk up.

He tossed his head towards the two ponies whose breakfast he had stolen. "I'll sort them out, just you see. Don't worry about it. When I'm around, everyone's a winner!"

Cobweb pranced round him in delight.

Lauren watched them, laughing. The gold and silver ghosts! Just wait till Tashy saw them . . . and the show on Saturday. She couldn't wait!

Chapter Seven

The Show

Riding to the show, the girls followed Tocker and Cobweb. The two ponies were invisible but the sound of their hooves rang out on the road. The girls knew the way, of course, but bossy Tocker insisted on showing that he remembered his way around as well. He got a bit confused when he came to a new roundabout, but blustered his way over the top, skipping round the cars, and the girls rode sedately round and met him on the other side.

"Funny thing to put in the middle of the road," they heard him say to Cobweb.

Everyone stared, hearing four sets of hooves making such a racket. But they were surprised to see only two ponies. Monkey and Humpfrey were very good in traffic, although the girls rarely rode on the roads. If Tocker hadn't been a ghost he would have caused several accidents before they arrived at the showground. He didn't believe in waiting for cars.

The show was quite a big one, bigger than the last. Horseboxes were lined up in rows. It was always difficult to find a bit of fence or hedge to tie up to, but the girls found a quiet spot under an oak tree. The Whitemarket horsebox was parked a little way down from them, and Lunar was already being ridden round by Shona-Ilona. He was so full of himself that she had to wear him out a bit to make him behave. Lauren's job was just the opposite: she had to wind Humpfrey up to make him go.

Shona rode past and said very rudely, "You haven't bothered to bring *your* ponies, have you?"

Tocker leapt out of the shade of the oak tree and barged straight into Lunar, so that Lunar shot sideways and Shona fell off.

She kept hold of the reins and bawled at Lunar, "You beastly pony!"

Tocker whickered with delight at his own tricks and Shona said to Lunar, "You're seeing ghosts, you stupid pony! What made you do that?"

When she had ridden on, Lauren heard Cobweb say rather severely to Tocker, "Don't make a spectacle of yourself. Behave!"

"I can't be a spectacle when no-one can see me," Tocker said, annoyed. But he was quiet after that, eating from other ponies' haynets and coming back every minute or two to say, "Can't we jump yet?"

At last they announced the first ponies' jumping class. In the collecting ring Shona was waiting on Lunar, and several well-known jumping ponies were walking around. Their riders stared in derision at Monkey and Humpfrey. Lauren and Tashy felt very nervous, wondering if their faith in Cobweb and Tocker was going to be rewarded. This class was for real, and they weren't sure what was real and what wasn't any more.

Lauren was more nervous because Humpfrey was old, and perhaps even with Cobweb and Tocker to help he might just not be up to it, or might hurt himself trying. They all knew that Monkey could do it if he wanted to, so bullying would work with him. Lauren was getting so nervous she wished she hadn't come. After all, nobody knew whether this plan was going to work. Tocker was so unreliable, not like dear Cobweb.

The class started.

It was a difficult course and there were

only two clear rounds before Lunar. Lunar went in and did the third clear.

The commentator said, "Clear round by this brilliant pony Lunar, who is never out of the ribbons. Next in . . ." you could hear his notes rustling . . . "Natasha Parks on Monkey." His voice changed, all the enthusiasm replaced by a sort of resignation, as if he was thinking, "We'll have to rebuild the course after this one."

Tashy looked white and terrified.

Monkey did his usual stupid prancing about as he went into the ring. But Cobweb was ahead of him – Lauren could see her but she knew no-one else could – and Monkey went after her. Tocker gave him a hard nip on the backside and he flew over the first jump. Tocker whizzed over at his side.

Together they went on to the second. With Cobweb and Tocker one on each side there was no way Monkey could run out or refuse. He just had to keep on jumping. And as his two companions jumped each jump with miles to spare, Monkey got the idea and did the same, jumping as if he had springs in his fetlocks. So high that the crowd started to laugh and clap.

The terribly good show-jumpers in the collecting-ring all stopped chatting and stared. Shona-Ilona dropped her reins and gawped.

Over the wall, over the double – bounce, bounce – like ballet dancers. And whizzing down to the last triple bar, which was really high . . . Lauren could see the light of excitement in Monkey's eyes as he stood off for the big jump. What a pony! He cleared it and landed nearly in the ropes, so huge was his jump. The crowd stood up and cheered and clapped.

The commentator, sounding amazed, said, "And that was Natasha Parks's Monkey – a clear round!"

Tashy rode back grinning all over her face. She patted Monkey and leaned down and put her arms round his neck. "See what you can do when you try! You wonderful pony!"

And then it was Lauren's turn.

She was so thrilled by Monkey's performance that she no longer felt any fear. Dear Humpfrey! Of course he was old and stiff and didn't really want to jump, but – just this once – with Cobweb and Tocker to bear him on their wings . . . Lauren had no fear.

She trotted into the ring.

And all of a sudden she felt Humpfrey turn into a *young* pony. He became supple and eager under her body and cantered towards the first jump as if on springs. What a feeling! Lauren's confidence soared as Humpfrey jumped.

Beside him Cobweb and Tocker flew through the air, their gold and silver dazzling her eyes. She was out in a new, magic world, taking jump after jump like an Olympic medallist, higher and higher! The old white pony was on wings, galloping and turning as agile as a rabbit, and leaving miles to spare over every obstacle.

Once more the crowd rose up and cheered and clapped. They had never seen a performance like the last two!

This time the commentator sounded quite faint. "And that was Humpfrey, ridden by Lauren Briggs. What a round!"

There had to be a jump-off. The jumps were made higher, and the three proper show-jumpers went in and did their rounds. They all knocked one or two down, including Lunar, who just clipped the top bar of the last triple jump. The pole teetered agonizingly, then fell.

Four faults!

And then Monkey.

Whizz, soar, whizz, soar . . . over and over like clockwork. There was not the slightest fear that he would make a mistake. And Humpfrey the same, the two girls finding out what it felt like to ride a really great pony. Dear Humpfrey, jumping for his life, all his stiffness vanished! But for his snow-white coat, he could have been a four-year-old again.

"The two have gone clear, Monkey and Humpfrey. Will they jump off again?"

"No, we'll share," said Lauren and Tashy.

Because they knew, however high the jumps went, neither of them would make a mistake.

They were both the winners.

They rode into the ring to take their rosettes, with Shona-Ilona trailing behind for her third, and the other two for their fourth and fifth. Shona-Ilona

Tashy rode away, but Lauren did not want to go home. Not yet.

She pinned her rosette up in the tack room. The one and only. Bright red, glowing in the gathering dusk like a great overblown rose.

Then she went down the field to say goodbye to Cobweb and Tocker. But when she got down to the bottom there were only two ponies there, Humpfrey and Monkey. They didn't even look up, but went on grazing happily.

Lauren stood looking. Her eyes filled with tears.

And on an off chance she walked on through the wood so that she could look down across the dunes to the sea. It was too great a day to go home yet; she didn't want it to finish. She didn't want to talk to anyone, or boast about her rosette. However could it be explained?

But when she got out of the shadow of the wood, she looked down towards

the beach. And there were Cobweb and Tocker, galloping across the sea-line side by side. The last red sliver of sun was just sinking below the horizon and the ponies were dark against the sun. Yet they glowed silver and gold, with a bright light all round them, and the spray they threw up glittered like diamond drops. They bucked with joy, and galloped faster and faster away down the beach, farther and farther

away. Their light faded into the dusk. Lauren watched until the last faint flicker disappeared. The beach was still and dark. She could just hear the murmur of the waves as they rolled steadily onto the shore. Nothing was any different. It was how it always was.

She stood there a long time, until she was cold.

She knew they wouldn't come back, but she waited all the same.

Then she went home.

On the way back she looked into the tack room. And the rosette was still there, pinned on the wall.

And she knew the rosette was real and wouldn't go away, not ever.

So she went home for her supper.

THE END